The Best Nest

Written by Isabel Thomas
Illustrated by Marc Pattenden

Jess has an egg but no nest!

Jetta has a nest.

Jinx has a nest.

Jem has a nest.

Jess has no nest!

Jess sprints on the sand.
She jumps across Zeb.

She trips up the fox!

Jess drops the eggs on the soft sand.

Talk about the story

Ask your child these questions:

1 What was Jetta's nest made of?

2 What was Jem's nest made of?

3 Why do you think Jess had no nest?

4 How did Jess save the day?

5 What type of bird do you like the most? Why?

6 What type of birds do you see near your home or school?

Can your child retell the story using their own words?